Wiles of Girlhood

Wiles of Girlhood

Joanne Arnott

PRESS GANG PUBLISHERS
VANCOUVER

Copyright © 1991 Joanne Arnott. All rights reserved.

This book may not be reproduced in part or in whole by any means without prior written permission from the Publisher, except for the use of short passages for review purposes. All correspondence to the author should be addressed to Press Gang Publishers.

Some of this work has previously appeared in *East of Main* (Pulp Press, 1989), *Monsters Aren't Real* (Women's Health Resource Collective, Australia, 1991), *Generation, (f.)Lip, Contemporary Verse 2*, and the *Carnegie Newsletter*.

Canadian Cataloguing in Publication Data
Arnott, Joanne, 1960-
   Wiles of girlhood

Poems.
ISBN 0-88974-034-8

I. Title.
PS8551.B67W5 1991   C811'.54   C91-091600-4
PR9199.3.A76W5   1991

First Printing October 1991
1   2   3   4   5   95   94   93   92   91

Cover art by Jo Cook, *Untitled,* Watercolour on rag paper, 77 X 58cm.
   Collection of the artist.
Cover design by Valerie Speidel
Book design and editing by Barbara Kuhne
Typesetting and production by V. Speidel
Typeset in Breughel; Linotronic output by The Typeworks
Printed on acid-free paper by Friesen Printing
Printed and bound in Canada

Press Gang Publishers
603 Powell Street
Vancouver, B.C.   V6A 1H2
Canada

for all the young women

*My sincere thanks to the many helpers, healers,
and companions I have found along the way.*

Contents

Wiles of Girlhood   11

Absences
    Absences   17
    flatland summer   18
    the war inside her   19

Con Sequence
    ThumbSketch, on Peace   23
    ThumbSketches II & III, Prairie Home   24
    Post-Attempt Confusion   25
    William's Wake   27
    Tender People in a Hard, Hard World   29

self/image   33

Crowning Sequence
    Devotion   49
    Umbilicus   52
    Change Herself   55
    Wrenching Life From the Ghosts   56
    Bitch & Destroyer   59

If Honour is Truth
    Pinion   63
    If Honour is Truth   64
    The Trail   65
    the lot of them   67
    Domain   68

Enter the Hard Place   71

Reprise
    Umbilicus   79

Double-Take
    A Poet Represents Her Poem   89

 Wiles of Girlhood

Wiles of Girlhood

GARBAGE

White paper, waxed stiff and shaped into a flat-bottomed cup, and used once, and crushed. Nearby, a lid, a cracked straw, mysteriously forged, equally abandoned. The eleven-year-old with her pain-hollowed face, her weedy dark hair, passed down the street with her eyes focusing inward.

ELEPHANT PANTS

She wore a very large pair of very bright pants, peacock blue, roped in at the waist so that uncomfortable bunches alternated with hanging crevasses, the whole shifting about with each step as her toes pulled the hems. Elephant pants. When anyone said, "What's that?" she ignored the laughter and answered, "These are my elephant pants."

THE FIGHT

They were halfway down to Dennis's, by the big hedge where she sometimes stopped to eat flowers. Small yellow flowers, honeysuckles she called them, with a tiny taste of sweetness among the petals. Or maybe the bush with the hard purple berries, said to be poison. Sam was with her, and when the large angry Prince bolted across the street toward them Sam stiffened and moved in a kind of pleasure to meet him. Their lips curled and their tails twitched in formal gestures, then both broke and lunged and they whirled fiercely together.

She waded in, telling them to stop. Their backs fell against her legs and launched forward again, totally absorbed, not listening.

Someone told her to move away, threw a bucket of water on them, shocking.

Flying

She walked down the street to school, tasting the rain and its relative freshness. On the way back up in the afternoon, she felt the wind at her back, and lifted her arms, arched her body. She knew there was a special way to do this, to send herself into the sky. She tried to, for it had a delicious sensation.

Phantoms

At night she was very concerned with a particular corner of the room. She threw all her concentration there, heard voices warbling in from another dimension. Wicked, angry voices, indistinct. Also a wee child's voice, she strained to hear it. None of these voices had bodies, faces. Invisible lives that would emanate from the blank shadows.

The Fire

She awoke to see the whole sky vivid and beautiful, and she could hear the operatic voices of the legions of angels. She ran to the window, with her sisters, and the eldest announced that it was a housefire down the street. "But what about the angels?" She shook her head, trying to shake the sound. But it remained, real, the singing.

Dysfunction

They were yelling in the kitchen, she had a bad sense of it, a foreboding. She moved past the tv set, along the wall where the guitars, ukelele, tambourines and drum were hung high, into the doorway as she heard the loud steps and the banging of the back door. Her father stood wiping the grease from the automobile from between his fingers. Her younger brother and sister stood separate before him.

His look of anger was overwhelmed with purest hatred, and he picked up a child and threw it against the wall, picked up the other and threw it at the same spot so that it fell on top of the other. Then he kicked and kicked the whole mess, shouting his fury.

Enchantment

There was a ghost that came in at night and tried to suffocate her older sister. It put a large hot hand that she said she could actually feel, right on her mouth, and a great weight pressing down all over her body. This was a very evil spirit, very frightening. Though it left, it might still come back to haunt her.

 Absences

Absences

midnights i feel
bludgeoned
by your deep
sleep   breath
           fires cackle
in my soul, my eyes
piercing the darkness
with wide light;

wednesday afternoons i sit
on concrete edgings
my feet   dabbing the tar
my eyes
mesmerized
by wheels turning
         i feel
cold drafts creeping
through my breasts
I hug them   tightly.

flatland summer

she sat there eating spiders
lamely off the walls
of inner tensions   pushing sliding
pulling taut and hang-
gliding through air
crunchy spiders
having nothing else to do
when the weeds
grow high around the porch
and the wind files in
from the old road pushing
at the house
solidly still   solidly still   the
elemental walls they
are outside and in   they can be
still and hot   they can be
cool and dim   cool and dim
and the echoes of the silence
running soft and low within
her empty head
crowded head
eyes of fullness

the war inside her

did you scent the war inside her, did you
hear the sound of bodies
falling from trees. did the sky
inside her appear glorious
and blue above the corpse-fed
beasts and vegetation. did the death there
scare you, were you
fearful as your gaze picked through
the grasses.
where did you run.
where did you run, do you know,
inside to the war-haunted forests and fields
or beyond, to the stern feeling
grey ungivingness
of concrete.

 Con Sequence

ThumbSketch, on Peace

ontariscape unrolling
rocks and hills, rocks and trees
ontariscape unwinding
bush and roads, sky and breeze
and billiam there beside me
boot and cap, laugh and squeeze
and billiam there beside me
bush and hills, rocks and trees.

ThumbSketches II & III, Prairie Home

tumble down through prairie,
scrub brush, hot fox on plain,
bright white silo burns blue sky,
tumble on, tumble
on

    saskatcheyellow,
    saskabruin, wilting
    green under sun,
    sun,
    sun over frost, over
    yapping yotes, over
    peace-stirring
    hitch-hikers

    (metallic
    flicks zip by,
    while i—
    still standing, eyes
    squint over distance,
    fingers
    browning with the curls
    of resinous smoke, heart
    pumping homeland
    to gentling scents of
    autumn free—)

    words
    of brother-love, and
    sister-love
    braid

    like land eating river
    over plain

Post-Attempt Confusion

because of you i scraped
the fine edge
of murder,
mostly, cruelly
mine,
so hard
heartfeltedly,
yours
  escape escape
  hotchkiss hotchkiss hotchkiss
  haunting — two nights

the web of madness spreads itself
wilder and wider
  breath of safety
  fear of peace, looking
  up and down the street

i am in search
of somestrong reality
beyond
  what is accepted
  what is perceived
  any and all that's
  lost between

in the rain i'm begetting
peace, forging
into fear and through to
coveted release;
    yes

silence trickles down
on a quiet night, bed
made and unmade
ready
for sleep

here i am then, safe,
soft presence in a
woman's home

there is pain there,
here,
inside:

a skeleton made
not to be so hard,
so rigid; a frame
made

for all the time fighting
is not

whatever i am

William's Wake

no. no. no! —
    take 'em out
and shoot 'em,
william said.

    william full of wonder
    pockets full of thunder
    tears the world asunder
    to take another view —

we'll have to track 'em,
he said.

    then all the world is new.

so how d'ya like that,
he screams, throttling me —
i can't live with ya
and i can't
live without ya

    struggle. choke. so
    kill me then — uh.
    bastard.
    uh.

so come on then.
so cold. out with the sob stories.
(what?) beg
for your life.

    william full of wonder
    i don't know what the situation is,
    so i don't know how
    to react.

don't be so stupid.

okay,
i'll trust you.

>	*bide my time. wait, and then*
>	*run or kill, something*
>	*final.*

(the jo chant, like
dreaming)—joanne
joanne joanne,
don't go,
don't leave me—

>	come talk to me.
>	talk to me—*then hard:*
>	stupid bastard.

don't go!
>	*william full of wonder*
don't go!
>	silence.
>	uh.
>	take 'em out
>	and shoot 'em.

Tender People in a Hard, Hard World

danger. parts of the
body go rigid, why
they are silently
asking each other, why
is it always a danger
in the air, why not
a thing
we can shoot, fight,
strangle...

persecution. i am laying
in a body of air or
water, cool and the flesh
between elbow and shoulder
is nibbled and stripped
by the hungry fish
piranha.

in a room, pale green
or blue, all about
crystal statues arranged
of eaglets. ten people
enter by various doors,
singly, and each
takes up a tiny eagle
and smashes to the ground
the silent symbol.
                    liberty,
we say, and learning to fly,
to be free.

is a cruel crock of shit.
the war goes on.

self/image

self/image

mirroring:

        her eyes were flat and
dark and dull. i wanted
to smash them   to let myself in
to let it all out, in more
than vapid echoes.

        stiff formless whispers, hush
        staccato on that plane
        behind the eyes. images
        jump and pulse and dance,
        sliding away before
        air might take might
        evaporate them, private
        husky visions.

thick mulled gaze barely
passing out of too still
face. the immobile
musculature that might
freeze into a smile
under complicated commands
of the hidden brain. that
too calm surface passing
as grace, that cardboard
figurine only assumed
to take place
as a multi-dimensional form.
that husk.
that representation.
a slow-moving symbol that must
thoughtfully be imagined
    a human being.

pre-stillness:

                    my body is restless i
cannot stay home any more.
my body is restless i
cannot stay home anymore.
each time

i step outside the house the world
invades me.
each time i take a step the
world can watch, my eyes
flame up and voice dies
in strangled whispers   mind goes
falling through the fibers of
my face.

how can i be so ugly.
how can i step outside for
the world to see, all my tangled
guts spill out
my face. my

shuddered form.
my fragile bodied storm
of broke emotion.

toward stillness:

                    the world is a dangerous
thorny-faced place. they
await you.
          welling up
out of their boredom they
nail you
tear at your skin   spitting
the unnamed angers and
icy-backed panic
in a stream
from their nerves to mine
from their taut nervous systems
to mine
from their unchecked gutless
loveless tentacled
tiny nerves,
to mine.

                yes i practised stillness. in pursuit
                of a way around
                a harmful gesture, a horrible
                word, in search
                of an impenetrable coat of
                feathers for
                protection, oh
                protection.

yes
i practised stillness. practised stillness
till i was blue
inside my face.

vampire-eyed, dog-tongued
bus drivers and factory workers, cooks
in restaurants, bikers
and punk-hoodlums, sleazy
businessmen in ties designed
not to strangle the wearer.
with their voices and their
slave block eyes
they persecute gently.
gently.

i cannot bear to be noticed.
i cannot bear to walk on the
empty streets, unseen
by others.
i float i drift i
peer in desperation, hoping
to link up to a gaze
that assures my existence.
i creep between rows of houses, down
city streets and i anguish

my ghost-like apparition needing
realization:
                    i skulk
when i see someone coming
        and then
i petrify.
they walk with eyes downcast
past the meaningless totem,
or they slow
and sloe-eyed stare, i am
typhooned all within
by anger, with terror. or else
they smile, and my face
churns open, and the ugliness
spills.

stillness.

where
is the passion the frenzy
of all humankind, where
the murder the batter the hotblood elopement
the sweat-stinging eyes wide-open to sex, where
is the heat
the easy-banked warm
the full-throated call
the dance i remember
where is the honest, the open, the friendship
where is the balance the centre the warm
where is the healthful
where is the loving
where is the truthful the giving outgoing
where the intelligence
where   curiosity, motion —

where is the peace?

                images. flicker. cluster. woman-
                heroes stride across her
                consciousness like
                meaning.
                her skin is false, ungiving;
                the images do not pass through,
                some of them die.

stillness.

for a lover:
                    i will invite you
before i permit myself
to take off the clothes,
to undo the bars, to dance
about the fire i've lit
in your favour (not
in my favour).
politely
i will invite you
i will
engage, direct, incite you   toward
the place upon this plane where
i become real.
            nobody
            gets there. i fail

to embody myself, yet
cannot desist from
invading you.

hysteria. it was not my womb
but my self, cut loose
uprooted and wandering aimless
inside my shell.

stillness:

        slap me slap me slap me
till i'm sane, blast me
hard enough to let me
rest assured of
my existence.

yes i practised stillness.

practised stillness till i was glued
inside my head, retreated far
to a tiny tender ledge
at skull's base.

how do i free myself now.

how do i shake off this form
it is excess baggage, coloured
like a target for the shooting
of poisoned arrows by
bored killers.
i am saturated,
still starving. gaunt-framed and
ghostlike unexpressed, i am still
a satiated vehicle. casual
receptacle.
how do i sever
myself from this form
it is binding me to a woman
each time
i open my ears
her virulent screams
inundate.

then when all the images
became death, months and years
of deadened attempting build
to an ultimate self-
disdain.

god-fucking coward.

incapable of the simple feat
of life, yet lacking
the one-shot necessary guts
required
to end it.

stillness breaks:

                stillness
breaks, the clotted need

spilling in webs and chunks, storming
all about the form, the face

is broken. body
screaming assertions, mind

spinning like chaos, the chains
melt into the limbs i use

to gather my sundered self
to a nearby cave.

the structure is fallen.
the armour come cage is
sprung open, and metal
leaks to the floor of the cave in
noxious pools.   the terror
beats to the surface of my skin, rage
and hatred mottles my limbs
my face my
breath
poisons the air with it. the
aggravated needing forms
a vacuum that
swallows the world.

i spit it out, retching.

stillness passing:

                the image of a great
                whole goddess
                rising
                within me.

i walk the broken pavement,
allowing the grey to show
upon my face.

i dip in the mud, i swim
down into the earth to seek out
my ancestors.
we flow together.

        the stature of a great
        whole goddess
        unfolds
        before me.

                the long limber
        and nondesperate limbs
        of the upright goddess.

        she strides the surface of the earth with
        unbowed shoulders,
        her head
        is strong boned and
        brown skinned,
        skimming through

silvering clouds
of
warming breath.

she listens:
i hear.

stillness passing:

                    the dishevelled and hollow
rebelliousness heals
into purpose. the reckless
wandering soothes
into a long and
blessed
journeying.

mirroring:

              i have seen those features breaking
as waves upon shore, the thick
the slow-moving earth
assaulted by the lithe and watery
waves, the moving
the transforming liquid
the splashing insistence
and the sullen earth moving
slow, in
lumbering grace, or
        quick in the crumbling shards of
fragmentation.

i have seen those features move.
i have seen
those features struggle and
die and grow hardened, and the pulsing
of life beat behind them and
break through the mask:
        off with the mould
        i love my flesh—

i have seen those features flow
liquid knowledge
spatial sense
the fiery warm that lives
and moves in earth's
dark secrets.
              fire in earth,
water in air i stand

in my naked human flesh.

the rain, the earth, the fire of me
are cleansing.

        the tactile
        presence
        of a Goddess

        looming
        behind me.

 Crowning Sequence

Devotion

1.

i want to unroll my life
on the flesh of the land, i want

to uphold the whole of womankind
on the flexible raft of my ribcage, warm

and strengthen her with my pride, feed
and nurture her at my breast which is

a mountain.

2.

the fire that drifts through your belly
drifts through me too, o earth and mentor:
if the blazes spill forth, scarring surface, who
cares, for it is fire that clears our route
of regeneration.

i have a stone mother, who is cold. her molecules
rub together like cows in the field, create
their own nurture. i don't want to be my mother,
her meditations the stillness of stone,
i want to overflow her peacefulness
with action.

3.

i want to move slow.
i want to flow a gentle course across
your womanflesh like the gathering rain,
and percolate down to your depths, nudging,
nuzzling my way through your folds and
the pores of your flesh, like the downpour
through grasses and soil.

i want you to rise like the early sun and
enlighten the fields with your fresh
new glitter. i want you to rise, already
imbued with me, and shine joyous.

Umbilicus

This is the place
where the rage came through.
A placenta pumping
powerlessness, placating.
Implicating.
With the first blood, webbing the spell
        of compromise.

Why should I forgive?
Under what guise
was I brought to this life, to provide
what kind of cloud, excuse
what weakness, be
whose burden so abandoned
at the root?

I shall be a ruthless mother
and an all-compelling self,
nonrighteous,
unstubborn,
true.

This is the place
where the rage came through.

Trying to kill that rage
was to withstand her absence.

Numbness wearing, and the trade
for her qualified presence

and love. She took me in
as I longed for her to do

when I came to her.
      What of   Demeter's love?

This is the place
where the rage came through

I have sought among women
for the touch of you

but no one has fought for my life
or come chasing after.

Now again I am pregnant,
this time with child.   I can choose of

two
worlds: one

where each child is
abandoned by her mother.

Or another, where a woman's commitment
              changes the earth.

        Why be kind?

However imperfect your back, I was formed
cupped at the base of your spine and
curled in your pelvis.
          However reticent your hand,

I have clasped it more than once
and pulled myself nearer your body,
nearer your mind.
                I scramble across you.
I leap from your shoulder.

But this is the place
where the rage came through.
I have hungered for a touch that is raw,
is new,

I have hungered for a strength
in myself and in you

why should I forgive?
under what guise
was I brought to this life?

to scour away
the empty pain
of no-commitment.

Change Herself

first my single woman's
scrawny form, taking on
roundness among the angles,
my single woman's mind explores
the meaning in being more—

where my borders are,
and the centre of balance,
pulled by unrelenting change,
secrets pulled from covert muscle
secrets leap with energy and blood
through opened channels,
flush about my being,
tumble out of disturbed flesh,
and materialize in dreams—

labour intensifies the process.
labour, the real shakedown—
birth
is terrifying—
for i cannot say no to the infant,
but to say yes
is to lay the mind open
to the whole of my unabsorbed life
stashed away in my body.

Wrenching Life From the Ghosts

o ghosts and demons
for fifty hours
i held you at bay
i held you at bay
for fifty hours
        in your chain mail fist
        in your hot stone mouth
        in your implacable grasp
        held tight, my infant

i wept, i remembered
the slashing phallus
of a lover; i allowed
my body to be used
be a rippling pool of pain
because of you, o ghosts
o demons
a chamber of pain
        you are a chained male fist
        you are a tongue and lips of stone
        you are a trap girding my hips
        who must be born
        for you are all wrapped up
        with my infant

o ghosts and demons
for twenty-five years
you've held me at bay
you've held me at bay
for twenty-five years
        with your hard and angry fist
        with your grinding teeth of stone
        with your clench upon my sex
        i fought you hard
        tore at myself to escape you
        ripped into flesh

i dreamt i remembered
the first time i flew
from my body. i was dropped
in the chasm of post-partum days
with a sick man and a child
slowly learning to breathe
suckle
defecate

i had to survive, so i
creased myself shut
banished the demon

ghost, fist, demon
holding the child
i am so disenchanted
i am so disenchanted
holding the child
    was i this young
    or how old, the first time
    you slammed into me
    fist
    o fist fist
    fist that split me in two
    and remains
    embedded
    always a threat
    holding me firmly in pieces

i am after you now
with a body, two bodies

one you leaped out of
another, my own

i will struggle
you down

wrench back
what is mine

i will
name you

Bitch & Destroyer

bitch and destroyer
brooding inside me
an elephant matriarch trumpeting
anger and grief

a belligerent moon
stamping off
across stars
trampling zodiac
heaving tides and blood
spewing light
spitting down silver
and ivory light
giving as i must give
to those who must take
and rasping
rasping the night

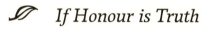 *If Honour is Truth*

Pinion

Laying in grass under poplar
green grass tickles my nose
my bones pressed to the hard earth
with the weight of time

turn another page, and shift
body against the ground
press fist into knotting belly
gag
lay my face down
into the story

If Honour is Truth

If I were a rat in a bucket
instead of your daughter,
would you take up the shovel just once,
killing me outright?

Few are the people whose smiles
I have sought with such rigour,
soaked in, treasured, like the rare
pure smiles alighting your face. And now

this long decade later, the distance
between us is finally a comfort,
not devastation. Bad boy, kicking his toy-like
offspring around rooms, into corners,

opting for tyranny in the home
instead of the harder inward struggle
that ends at peace. Your mistake lay
in thinking you could escape

dealing directly with your pain.
A bad boy, pushing his fears
and rage onto children, and *mastering*
them.

For children grow.
Having escaped the confines
of your psyche, and becoming the terrifying
outside world, we are approaching.

If you were a wild dog
instead of my father,
how many times would I try to befriend you,
before shooting you down?

The Trail

We share. We trade places.
We always try to be good.

Seven scared girls
listen for the tinkle
of its talons
on the hardwood floor.

We share.

Dragged itself out of the furnace
scratched across the coalbin
and escaped —

We trade places.

Reptilian drag
through the belly of the house —

We always try to be good.

Finally
pulled free of the chimney,
was gone — but the trail
it left...

We share.

Anger like a dragon
in each child's bowels...

We trade places.

Fear was all the sleepless children
in our bellies...

We always try

And when the dragons shake free
of the furnace, try
to ascend, we clamp down on them.

to be good.

Overturn the coalbins
of our memories.

the lot of them

i can remember
the lot of them
standing around the hole
in the floor
concerned
looking down
my father hoisting
the naked pale
body of my sister
up
out of the bare earth
out of the root cellar
into the house

i can remember
the lot of them

i can remember
moving stiffly away
tight
rigid with anger

Domain

sitting on a park bench,
my body unfurls itself as if
it were my father's, on a couch,
fingers lead arms out across the long
domain;
this is all mine, the body says,
knuckles brushing the furthest edges
of space

 **Enter the Hard Place**

Enter the Hard Place

I am lost, not lost but
overwhelmed with the fear
of becoming
lost
becoming
lost
might be
not coming back
might be
not coming back
to alive again
this is a place
without
this is a place
without
starlight
without
moonlight
without
sunlight
light in your eyes
i cannot see
i will not see
i am afraid

I am loss, not loss but
overcome with the fear
of begetting
loss
begetting
loss
might be
not getting back
might be
not getting back
to alive again
this is a place
within
this is a place
within
my bodymind
within my younger mind
within my mother's mind
in my son's eyes
i cannot get in
i will not get in
I am afraid

Where
is the squashed
girl?

where, where
in reality
where
within me
where
within the enchantment

when did i bury
this girl
where
did i bury her
where
did i bury her

is she alive?

is she dead?

is it safe now?

How much
does she know?
how much
am i willing
to know
how much
can i take
how much
can i bear

this
this is
this is it
this is my story
this is

my life

I enter
the hard place

I enter the hard place   I
am afraid

I told you

I said
I cannot see
but I told you
what it looks like
I told you
what it feels like
to be here

I asked you questions
you cannot answer them
I will answer them

Wait
for me

 *Reprise*

Umbilicus

This is the place
where the rage came through

a placenta pumping
powerlessness

placating
implicating

with the first blood
webbing the spell

of compromise

Under what guise
was I brought to this life

to provide
what kind of cloud

excuse
what weakness

be
whose burden so abandoned

at the root

I shall be a ruthless mother
and an all-compelling self

nonrighteous
unstubborn

true

This is the place
where the rage came through

trying to kill that rage
was to withstand

your
absence

numbness wearing
and the trade

for your qualified presence
and love

You took me in
as I longed for you to do

when I
came to you

What of
Demeter's love

This is the place
where the rage came through

I have sought among women
for a touch of you

but no one has fought
for my life

or come
chasing after

Now again I am pregnant
this time with child

I can choose
of

two
worlds: one

where each child is
abandoned by her mother

or another
where a woman's commitment

changes the earth

My belly is swelling
there is no end to this

over
and over

A limb that is not quite mine
rippling surfaces

body and mind
I am all moving over

all of me
moving over

all of some body
unknown

growing
inside me

growing
alone

but completely
within my domain

new flesh
new bone

rolling in a sea of rhythm
pulsing placenta

pulse of breath
and of heart

Persephone Demeter
Demeter Kore Demeter

Persephone Kore Persephone
Demeter

There are many ways of looking
at the rape of a daughter

the loss
of a mother

the movement
from body to body to body

across
the Triple Goddess

in this life

However imperfect your back
I was formed

cupped at the base of your spine
curled in your pelvis

However
reticent your hand

I have clasped it
more than once

pulled myself
nearer your body

nearer
your mind

I scramble
across you

I leap
from your shoulder

But this is the place
where the rage came through

I have hungered for a touch
that is raw

is
new

I have hungered
for a strength

in myself
in you

to scour away
the empty pain

of no-commitment

 *Double-Take*

Double-Take:
A Poet Represents Her Poem

Before giving birth and exploring the whole transformative process of pregnancy and birth, I had a miscarriage and two abortions. On the occasion of my second abortion I wrote the poem "Abortion (Like Motherhood) Changes Nothing." The title reflects my mother's opinion of motherhood, and the hope she passed on to her daughters that non-motherhood would provide a healthier alternative for us, to her experiences as a Roman Catholic, working-class wife and mother. The first sentence came to me while I was walking down the street. It is this: "I am a cunt, and the folds of my face are purple." That is the point of view taken in the poem. It is a cynical rebuttal of my mother's hopes.

> ABORTION (LIKE MOTHERHOOD) CHANGES NOTHING
>
> I am a cunt, and the folds of my face
> are purple. My mouth, delicate and moist,
> a pale pink.
> Like your tongue, like the roof
> of your mouth my throat
> arcs gently, while
> all around me pulses
> my heart (the pump
> of power, the vibrant
> juices). At the base of my throat
> is an organ, the organ
> is growing, it swells
> from lemon to orange to melon
> as the long days pass. Here
> at the base of my throat
> life and death are meeting
> for a hot red time.

> Life and death are meeting
> at the base of my throat, i do not
> scream, i do not
> gurgle. Life and death
> are cavorting, and when
> all is done,
> receding,
> both of them, all of us,
> back down the throat to
> the lip of my face,
> out into the world
> of men—
>
> off to
> meander again.
> The organ forgotten reduces
> to her virgin size; my self
> slips back to the usual
> uncondensed form;
> and my cunt,
> she is returned to
> a shadowy half-known place,
> off along
> the tenuous edge
> of being.
> My face
>
> remembers her eyes, her nose
> and ears, her taste buds.
> My face
> speaks well, again, in places, in that
>
> stilted *human* tongue.

I wrote that in 1985.

Shortly thereafter, I became engaged in another bout with fertility. I describe the experience in "Umbilicus": "now again I am pregnant,/this time with child." While I was exploring this pregnancy process, the women in my family began for the first time to really acknowledge consciously, and to one another, that incest and violent sexual abuse is intrinsic to our shared family experiences. Coming to consciousness individually, and as a group, has required an amazing degree of persistence and has released huge amounts of energy, often as rage. Although I remember only pieces of a life, I know now that I am a sexual abuse survivor.

Turning to this poem again with this revived consciousness, what I hear is a loud, protesting voice from the other side of forgetting, the other side of occlusion, the part of myself who will never hesitate to say precisely *what is*.

Listen again to some of the words:

> I am a cunt...
> . . . .
> ... my throat
> arcs gently, while
> all around me pulses
> ... the pump
> of power...
> At the base of my throat
> is an organ, the organ
> is growing...
> . . . .
> Life and death are meeting
> at the base of my throat...
> scream...
> gurgle...

Clearly the knowledge bleeding through is that of oral rape.

The rest of the poem portrays the process of occlusion, forgetting, and its consequences. I say we "recede," that the "organ" is "forgotten." I describe the world as one "of men," my movement through it "meandering." I describe my return to my body/senses, to a "usual" though still rather disembodied state of being. The ending is as much about this second, inner reading as it is about abortion; the awareness of occlusion is plain:

> My face
> speaks well, again, in places, in that
> stilted *human* tongue.

On both levels of this work I damn the agreed-upon reality, acknowledging the huge chunks of our lives that are denied place and consciousness within that construction. The unheard of and denied become literally the unthinkable, no matter how many times we experience them. What remain are potent gaps in our personal and collective memories, knots of tension in our bodies and communities, and free-floating, random images of fear. This experience of dissonance is, for most of us, fundamental.

All of this poem was written, reworked, and revised without ever tilting the balance of memory/nonmemory, knowing/not knowing. It took a few more years and the continued interaction with others before that balance began to shift.

It is not true that we are individual. In body and mind, we are endlessly divisible, and we do become divided when our experiential worlds and the spoken, agreed-upon reality are consistently incongruent. Nor is it true that we are alone in this world; isolation is one of the greatest tools used to disempower people(s), and within the cult of the individual we as people, as communities, remain fragmented.

We are forged by this culture at the same time that we are its living tendrils. We create this culture too, consciously and unconsciously, in our best and our worst moments. In acknowledging the splits within ourselves, and between us, by locating the potent gaps and making space for them to materialize—by realizing them—we undermine the dissonance. We make sense, for ourselves, for everyone.

photo: Dorothy Elias

JOANNE ARNOTT was born in Manitoba in 1960 and was raised in various urban and rural communities in western Canada. She studied English at the University of Windsor, Ontario, and in recent years her writings have been published in a number of feminist and literary magazines. *Wiles of Girlhood* is her first book.

Now living in Vancouver's downtown eastside, Joanne is the mother of two sons, Stuart and Harper, and lives with them and their father/her partner, Brian Campbell. She facilitates Unlearning Racism workshops as a member of the alliance group, A.W.A.R.E., and is currently working on her second book. *My Grass Cradle* will focus on erasure, regionality, and her mixed Native and European ancestry.

Jo Cook is a painter and set designer living on Mayne Island, British Columbia. Her paintings, drawings and woodcuts have graced the covers of many publications, including *The Fairies Are Thirsty* by Denise Boucher, *The Animals in Their Elements* by Cynthia Flood, and issues of *Room of One's Own*, *Quest* and *Makara*. Cook's work has been shown in over twenty exhibitions, including a major retrospective at the Surrey Art Gallery in 1988.

Press Gang Publishers Feminist Co-operative is committed to publishing a wide range of writing by women which explores themes of personal and political struggles for equality.

A free listing of our books is available from Press Gang Publishers, 603 Powell Street, Vancouver, B.C. V6A 1H2 Canada